The Authority Accele Blueprint:

The 100 Day Plan for Entrepreneurs, Business Owners, Authors, Experts and Speakers to Grow Their Business, Brand and Exposure

by

John A McCabe

Dedication

This book is dedicated to…
My parents, Gary and Shirley McCabe, whose guidance throughout my life was everything that was needed. They taught me to work hard, be honest, and follow my dreams.

My best friends, Heather Morrow and Jeff Wade, who have always been there for me. They supported me in my ups and my downs and when I was penniless and homeless, they were there offering me a place to stay, food and some financial support so I could continue to pursue my dreams. They offer their unconditional love and support.

Thank you to all my clients for believing in me and making this possible.

Acknowledgement

This book couldn't have happened without so many people that I need to thank. First and foremost are my wonderful parents, my mom Shirley and father Gary. My amazing friends Heather and Jeff who are always there to support me in both the good times and the bad.

My COACHES, Ed Rush and Mike Koenigs, who have always offered their support, guidance and wisdom throughout the years.

My CLIENTS who given me the opportunity, time and help to get this book completed.

I am deeply grateful to everyone who stood by me and believed. I thank all in my personal and professional circles who influence me. I thank my editor, Jennifer Schimmel. I especially thank my clients who are using these strategies to achieve unstoppable growth in their businesses.

Contents

About the Author

Three-time International #1 best-selling author, speaker, entrepreneur, business coach, consultant and real estate investor, John A. McCabe, has been helping entrepreneurs and businesses since 2004.

John has an impressive career as both a business consultant and real estate investor. Through his implementation of process, procedures, systems, technology, and personnel, he helped grow a company from $1.5 million to $7 million in just four years while dramatically increasing its bottom line.

John then started ioffersolutions Real Estate Services and within two years had been involved in controlling over $10 million worth of real estate, generating him a six-figure-per-year income without ever using his own money or credit. As a proud entrepreneur, John built his business by generating an abundance of leads and opportunities. By positioning himself and his business as the go-to company in the field of Rent To Own, he is now a recognized authority in assisting people stop foreclosure.

Taking what has made him so successful in his business ventures, John has developed a formula that, when implemented, consistently yields results.

Originally from Windsor, Nova Scotia, the Birthplace of Hockey, he studied business at Acadia University then moved to Edmonton, Alberta, where he currently lives and works.

John gives credit to his parents, Gary and Shirley McCabe, his Business Coaches Ed Rush and Mike Koenigs, along with inspiration from Gary Vaynerchuck.

John enjoys fast-pitch softball and has won numerous provincial championships, and has competed at both the national championships and the ISC World Fastball Championship. He now spends his spare time golfing and travelling.

Follow the Author

You can follow John A. McCabe through his social media accounts.

- Facebook.com/JohnAnthonyMcCabe

- Facebook.com/TheJohnAnthonyMcCabe

- Facebook.com/ The.Authority.Accelerator

- Twitter.com/JohnAMcCabe

- Youtube.com/user/JohnAnthonyMcCabe

- Linkedin.com/in/TheJohnAnthonyMcCabe

- Google.com/+JohnMcCabe

- Instagram @JohnAMcCabe

- Snapchat @TheJohnAMcCabe

FREE Video

Authority Acceleration Formula

www.AuthorityAcceleratorCoach.com

About This Book

Every once in a while, a revolutionary idea, system, model or formula comes along that completely transforms the landscape of an industry.

This book is not your traditional marketing book, but rather addresses the number 1 problem every single entrepreneur, business owner, author, expert and speaker has right now... getting ATTENTION!

My guess is you're here right now because you have a mission, a purpose, and a desire for a lifestyle change, control over what you do and how you do it. You're here because you want to dramatically grow your business, your brand, your income, exposure, serve more people or make a bigger impact in people's lives.

I know what that feels like. It's why my passion has always been to help people grow their business by attracting more attention, generate leads and opportunities to get you out there following up, closing deals and making more money. If this sounds like you, then you're in the right place at the right time!

What if there was a way to get you seen, heard, noticed, anywhere, at any time on any device, while becoming a best-selling author and have a successful podcast channel? What if you could make it happen within 100 days only spending 1 hour per week on content creation?

This book will introduce you to a strategic formula that creates an impact on your ideal target market, position you as the expert or authority in your business or field of expertise, and accelerate your ability to give value and deliver deeper value to those who want your help.

By the time you finish reading this book and reviewing some of the FREE resources, you'll understand the underlying strategy behind the "Authority Acceleration Formula" and have a blueprint that will assist you in implementing the Formula into your business.

Preface

Welcome, my name is John A. McCabe and I'm going to walk you through the "Authority Acceleration Blueprint", which is the execution of the "Authority Acceleration Formula" over the next 100 days, positioning you as the Go-To Expert or Authority in your business and field of expertise.

Now, I realize that is a big and bold claim, and I want you to be skeptical. Having said that, I can promise that when you spend some time with this book, companion videos and join the Facebook Group, you'll see just how easy it can be to grow your business, brand, income, expertise, serve more people and make a bigger impact in people's lives.

Since 2009, I've been growing, building, tweaking and perfecting a system for my own personal business that generates my business an abundance of leads and opportunities. In the summer of 2016, I made the conscious decision that I wanted to model the leaders I was looking up to and following. I wanted to be my own version of people like Mike Koenigs, Ed Rush, Gary Vaynerchuck, Ryan Deiss, Frank Kerns, and so many others. I knew, and still know that my unique perspective, skillset and experiences allow me to think differently than most people. I have a great deal of experience and a diverse background that is extremely useful when dealing with different business and overcoming their challenges. I have learned from some of the best to bring out the best in me.

So, I decided that starting August 29th, I was going to commit myself to being recognized as an authority in the field of Coaching, Consulting and Advising for entrepreneurs, business owners, authors, experts and speakers around the world on how you can accelerate your authority in 100 days or less.

This was something I had actually done before in the Canadian Real Estate Investing business niche I was known for. Now I'm venturing into a bigger playing field so I needed to start from scratch, just like every one of you have done in your business.

December 6th, happened to be 100 days from the time I started. Now that 100 days will come back into play shortly, but in the 100 days from the time I started implementing my formula I was standing on the stage at a major marketing event called Go Live and Profit. I was asked to speak because I successfully implemented my formula, conducted about 70 one hour Facebook Live shows in that 100 days, and gained exposure to new audiences and people who previously had never heard of me.

From the 70 hours of video footage I created by going Live 5 days a week for 100 days, I have enough content to create 7 books, which are all under way (this being 1 of the 7), 70 audio and video podcast shows, hundreds and hundreds of video clips, posts, tweets, images etc. for a variety of social platforms using a number of different mediums. All designed to do one thing… get me more ATTENTION and grow my business!

Now one thing I need to make clear, you don't need to invest 5 hours a week doing a live show. It's actually overkill and will eat up much of your valuable time. You can have an amazing impact with only 1 hour per week of live content, which I will get into more detail later when I break down the "Authority Acceleration Formula".

Imagine, spending just 1 hour per week over the next 100 days and having enough content to create all the authority positioning resources such as a Live Show, Best Selling Book, Podcast channel and an abundance of social posts that will get you seen, heard, recognized, anywhere, anytime on any device as the Authority or go-to person in your business or field of expertise.

Even if you've read other marketing books, this one is different because it isn't all theory. This book provides you with some background theory, but also a very strategic plan to implement and track during a 100-day time period in order to accelerate your authority in your business and field of expertise.

If you use what's here, it will forever change the way you are viewed with respect to your industry. More people will start to come to you for information and help, which generates more leads, opportunities and business.

I know you may be super busy, overwhelmed or simply looking for ways to get ahead. My guess is you want a lifestyle change, more control over what you do and how you do it... You want to serve more people, make more money, spend more time with family and friends and travel more... and maybe you're just getting started....

The first thing you should do is go to www.JohnAMcCabe.com and get access to all the FREE Videos I've created about the program and The John A McCabe Show. When you register for the free videos, you'll also get notified when this book is updated. It's a work in progress and will change based on the feedback and comments I receive.

Next, attend one of our "Master classes" – high-quality, interactive online events. When you register for the free videos, you'll be registered automatically and receive an invitation link to join me. There, you'll meet me and have a chance to learn more about everything we talk about in this book firsthand with live-chat and interactivity. These Master classes are fun and you'll learn a ton.

When you apply the content in this book and the FREE resources you have access to, you will be positioned as the expert or authority in your business or field of expertise relatively quickly.

Everything in this book works – in fact, it is constantly evolving and being refined. I built my coaching business around these strategies and systems from start to finish in just 100 days. Similar strategies are being used successfully by thousands of others all over the world. It can work for you too.

Here's a warning: Don't delay. Take imperfect action. The Internet, the web and social media are growing at an amazing pace. The world will continue to get more competitive; people will feel even more overwhelmed and get busier. Right now, it's easier and more affordable than ever before to be seen, heard and found.

But that might change a day, a week, a month or a year from now and the sooner you get started and implement the strategies found in "The Authority Acceleration Blueprint," the faster you can accomplish your dreams.

Enjoy this book and the videos and I will see you on the other side of the screen.

John McCabe

Section 1: Foundation

FOUNDATION

----

foun·da·tion
noun

an underlying basis or principle for something.
"this idea is the foundation of all modern marketing"

synonyms: basis, starting point, base, point of
departure, beginning, premise;
principles, fundamentals, rudiments;
cornerstone, core, heart, thrust, essence,
kernel
"the report has a scientific foundation"

FREE Video

Authority Acceleration Formula

www.AuthorityAcceleratorCoach.com

Chapter 1: Expectations

EXPECTATION

----

ex·pec·ta·tion
noun
plural noun: **expectations**

a strong belief that something will happen or be the case in the future.

"what expectations do you have for your future? "

synonyms:
anticipation, expectancy, eagerness, excitement, sus
pense
"tense with expectation"

There is a good chance that if you are reading this book you are an entrepreneur, business owner, author, expert or speaker and you're looking to dramatically grow your business, your brand, your income, your exposure, serve more people or make a bigger impact in people's lives.

This book will help position yourself as the authority in your business or field of expertise – fast. Whether you already have a successful business or you are just getting started, this is a strategy for getting seen, heard, noticed, anywhere, anytime on any device, and get the attention of the people who are looking for the products or services you offer.

Think about it – what if people started to come to you specifically for your help? Knowing already what it is that you do, who you help and how you help them and want to work with you. Money in hand. When you implement the strategies laid out in this book and the Authority Acceleration Blueprint, that is exactly what you will have.

There is a process, a method, a formula if you will, that can get you there. I've created and honed this formula since 2009, and I'm going to share it with you in this book.

Everything I'm going to teach you is based on real-world results and is working right now in today's internet world. This method was created through trial and error, a huge investment into learning which strategies work and which ones don't, and real-life experience.

The results have been staggering. I re-invented myself after years in the real estate investing space. Within 100 days, I was standing on stage at a major marketing event for people doing business online, giving a talk about the same strategy I'm going to share with you in this book. To watch that 15 minute presentation, visit http://www.AuthorityAcceleratorCoach.com

Not only did I make my way on to a major marketing stage, but I was introduced to countless new audiences, made several new connections and I'm doing business with individuals that I would never have met if I had not implemented this strategy into my business.

The funny thing is, as I reflect back, it happened almost as I knew it would. I started implementing my formula and quickly become a leader in my field of expertise. In fact, when I started out, I was entering into a big new pond, where I had very little credibility. I knew I had to make something happen fast while at the same time overcome my obstacle of being an introvert. I experienced anxiety at just the thought of cold calling people or knocking on doors trying to get business. There were some definite stretch goals.

The "Authority Acceleration Blueprint" method is comprised of 4 main components and it's important for you to understand them before running off and starting your 100-day plan.

In this first section of the book I will get into the first three components, which make up the foundation stage of the blueprint. This is where you get to understand the overall strategy and lay the groundwork for your business. You refine your message so it resonates with those you want to attract and do business with.

In the second section of this book, known as the execution stage, I will dig into the last two interactive components of the Blueprint. This is where you map out and execute "Authority Acceleration Formula" over a period of 100 days to get seen, heard, and noticed. And in doing so, you will build your business, your brand, your income, your exposure, serve more people and make a bigger impact on people's lives.

Chapter 2: Impact

IMPACT

----

im·pact

verb

im'pakt/

have a strong effect on someone or something.

"high interest rates have **impacted on** retail spending"

synonyms: affect, influence, have an effect on, make an impression on;
hit, touch, change, alter, modify, transform , shape
"high interest rates have impacted retail spending"

Every single person reading this has the power to generate ATTENTION and create an IMPACT. I'm not saying that to be cliché. Now more than ever you really have the power to be recognized and to change the world with your unique talents, gifts, products and services.

In your hand, in your pocket, in your purse, each and every one of you has the most powerful device known to man for getting attention, getting more exposure, and being recognized around the world... and that's your smartphone.

So a single video, tweet, picture, post from your phone can start a ground swell. An idea or thought you have for a segment you serve, a story you share, it could be the start of something huge, and it can actually re-write your future. But that idea, thought, story is powerless if it stays inside of you. If you never share that information out to others, it will wither inside of you, just as your business and dreams of financial freedom will never reach their full potential.

Now maybe you have tried to share your information with others, only not to be noticed. And it's even worse, someone with a far less superior product or service, has theirs adopted or purchased. And the biggest reason is that people didn't know who you were and why they should listen to you in the first place.

If you communicate your idea in a way that resonates with the people you are trying to IMPACT, and you position yourself to be everywhere they are turning when they're searching from their homes, their offices, their bedrooms and yes... even their bathrooms as a welcome guest, then change will happen. You will be able to effect change and IMPACT the lives of the people who need your help the most.

I've been attending large marketing events since 2011, and I've been in rooms of upwards of a thousand people. During all that time, going to events just like many of you have attended, the number of people I've interacted with on a personal level is very small.

Now it isn't that I'm anti-social, that I'm overly shy, that I feel superior in anyway whatsoever... far from it. It's because I'm an introvert and I know how to respond to various scenarios. Participating in multiple full day events drains my energy. I'd rather listen and observe in a group of people rather than constantly be interacting with others or be the person who thrives on sharing their thoughts to the group.

When I attend those events, I'm doing my recon ahead of time. Where are the washrooms? How many exits are there? Where is the best place for me to sit and come and go without being noticed? Where are the quiet sitting areas in the lobby where I can go and recharge when needed?

Now don't get me wrong, I do socialize and I tend to make some great connections and consider people to be friends in the community. And it seems that every event I go to I make one or two more.

But the beautiful part of doing anything online, even live video is that there is a space between myself and the audience. And I'm actually more comfortable talking on stage in front of hundreds of people than I am interacting in a group of 5-10 people.

And when one of my mentors started livestreaming before livestreaming was even cool, I was right there with him. I knew it was a way that I could get my message out to the masses without having to take myself too far outside my comfort zone.

But getting your message out to the masses so you can reach more people is work. It won't happen with just one livestream, video, image or post. That information has got to spread… or it won't be effective. So, it has to come out of you, and out into the open in a variety of different mediums, on a number of different platforms and on a consistent and persistent basis for it to IMPACT people and have them engage and share it with others.

However, before you start sharing your message, it is very important you get clear on that message, who you are going to talk to, what their current struggles or desires are, how you can help them and what benefits they would receive from working with you. All of which I will discuss in the upcoming chapters.

FREE Video

Authority Acceleration Formula

www.AuthorityAcceleratorCoach.com

Chapter 3: Authority

AUTHORITY

----

au·thor·i·ty
noun

the power to influence or command thought,
opinion, or behavior

"he had absolute **authority over** the people in the
audience"
synonyms: power, jurisdiction, command, control, ch
arge, dominance, rule, sovereignty, supr
emacy;
influence;

As I discussed in the previous chapter, reaching more people and IMPACTING others can be challenging. You need your message to reach others and for them to want to listen to what you have to say and feel that your message is speaking directly to them. This is easy once you are already recognized as someone who has credibility, expertise or authority.

For most, they don't feel they can be a recognized authority for a variety of reasons. What these people fail to realize is that being the authority doesn't mean you have the most experience, have the most education, have the biggest business or client base, how well you are currently known or even being best in the marketplace. Being the Authority generally means you are recognized for having 2 very specific components:

1. You have a core competence in your business or field of expertise

2. You are committed to serving others with your unique talents and gifts

Becoming the authority in your business or field of expertise is about positioning yourself as the go-to person in your industry. People take notice of you, get to know you, like you and trust you. Let's face it, people do business with people they know, like and trust.

But how do you get there, especially if you are just starting out?

There are 2 parts you should consider before starting on your journey to become the authority in your field of expertise. The first – what can you do that will give you "perceived" authority even if none exists? Second – how can you craft your message so it resonates with people and gets them to listen, take notice, share, engage and follow what you have to say?

For this chapter, I'm going to use myself in all the examples. I want to give as much transparency to the process and I can provide much more disclosure about myself versus my clients' experiences here. I also want to modal for you that as an entrepreneur, it is more and more important to be vulnerable and put yourself out there. I need to do what I proclaim if I want to impact change to the people I serve.

What you will notice is how I've been able to quickly position myself as an Authority in the area of helping my clients get seen, get heard, get noticed and deliver a message that resonates with who they're trying to attract. This makes it much easier for people to want to do business with you, and changes the power dynamic so you aren't scrambling to find clients, but rather, people are scrambling to work with you.

Authority Quick Start

If you're just starting and don't have much experience, any or many results or accomplishments that illustrate who you are, who you help and how you help them, then you can leverage related experiences in other fields, jobs, volunteer work that can transfer and demonstrate the kind of person you are and the skillset you have.

Another great way is for you to borrow authority from others by proximity. This is also called "Authority by Association". This means you find people who are considered experts or authority figures in your field of expertise and get your picture taken with them, interview them and even get testimonials from the people the market knows.

Authority by Association

When I started my business of Canadian Real Estate Investing, I invested a great deal of money into courses, masterminds and coaches in the field of marketing. As a result of successfully implementing many of the marketing strategies I've learned, I have had the opportunity to speak and be part of panels at the same events as these well-respected people in the marketing industry. Because of that I can make the following statement...

"I've shared the stage with marketing experts and influencers like Mike Koenigs, Ed Rush, Mike Filsane, Pam Hendrickson, Lisa Sasovich, John Assaraf just to name a few."

Now just from that statement, you can see I'm putting myself in the company of some very well-known people in the area of marketing. So even before I ever got started in my new field of expertise, I am able to create some authority for myself by proximity.

Think about any talks, discussions, events you were at where you were able to participate with some well-known people in your field of expertise. Did you speak at the same event? Were you ever on the same show or interviewed by the same person? If not, try to find a situation where you can create this opportunity for yourself.

Now, let's take a look at some of the things I've accomplished in my past and how I can show why they provide value to others and how I can use them for my Authority Positioning.

Accomplishments

Prior to getting into Real Estate Investing in 2009 I worked for myself as an independent Business Management Consultant in the field of Business Operations.

From 2004-2009, I had 1 client in the field of Industrial Sandblasting and Painting industry based on Nisku, Alberta that I worked on 40-60 hours per week, except for a 6-month hiatus.

My accomplishment as an independent consultant is that I helped grow that company from 1.5M to 7M in just 4.5 years by implementing processes, procedures, streamlining operations, implementing technology, scheduling systems, project management philosophy, identifying individuals for key positions and much more within the organization.

This demonstrates my ability to:
- take a high level view of an organization

- evaluate the operations

- identify key areas that lack efficiency

- create, implement and execute changes within the organization that have a positive impact on the company's revenues and expenses

Most companies require the same fundamentals when it comes to business; however they all have minutiae differences and nuances. Most strategies can be implemented into various businesses regardless of their industry and still be effective.

When I went to consult the sandblasting and painting business I knew absolutely nothing about the business of sandblasting and painting. I had come from the corporate world of payroll processing, software systems and project management. Fortunately, much of what I learned about systems, project management and technology was transferable to other businesses.

By taking the role of the observer, asking questions, watching people and the operations of the company as a whole for the first week, I was able to identify which areas had the largest room for improvement and the biggest impact on the bottom line. I then went ahead and implemented the strategies, systems and philosophies into the business that made an immediate impact in the business.

In the very first month of a business that was grossing $1.5M per year, most of it in a 6-month window, I was able to add $50,000 to their bottom line NET figure just from implementing strategies I learned in my other career. I increased their yearly Net Income by

3.33% in just one month! For a company that was going in the RED each winter, that was huge.

I created a domino effect within the company. The increase efficiency enabled them to make more money, push through more projects, give the workers steady work, decrease labor costs, increase productivity, make more money, build their own state of the art facility, and then increase everything all over again. Even expand into other markets.

This example hopefully gets my point across: Many of the skills you have, and accomplishments you've achieved in your past, can play a big part in your Authority Positioning. When you're first getting started in your new business or field of expertise, this is an effective strategy.

Now, let me bring this back to the context of positioning myself as an Advisor, Coach, Consultant in the field of Accelerating Your Authority. My background accomplishments of implementing strategies, systems and blueprints to dramatically grow a company over a very short period of time added massive credibility to myself in a Business Field where I was just getting started.

Helping you Accelerate Your Authority in 100 days or less comes down to implementing a very specific system, strategy, blueprint or formula. I've already demonstrated in that one example I have the ability to create and implement systems that can have an immediate impact on a business in the short term, as well as grow it in the long term.

Therefore, the question for you is: What transferrable skills and accomplishments do you have that can be used if you are just getting started in a new business or field of expertise? For those who have been in your industry for some time and want to position yourself as the authority, then show or talk about examples of helping your ideal target market achieve their desired outcome.

The skills you have that are directly related to the field of expertise or industry you are going into is much easier to link with accomplishments.

My goal is to help you generate exposure and awareness in a very short period of time so you can generate more sales, make more money and make a bigger impact in people's lives. You might be thinking... "Ok John, where's your authority in being able to do this? Where is your authority in the field of creating and accelerating authority for someone or a business?"

For this example, we are going to take a look back at my real estate investing business. In the recession of 2009, I was given 1-day notice that my services with the sandblasting and painting business would no longer be required. I had been self-employed for about 7 years and times were tough. Consultants and even employees weren't getting hired in my field of expertise at that time. Fortunately, I had just taken 3 real estate investing training courses so I decided to give that a try. However, I had 1 big issue... I am an introvert. There was no way I was going to cold call people or knock on doors to try to convince homeowners they needed my service. In addition, that modal would not yield the revenue potential I needed right out of the gate.

I had to figure out how I was going to get people to contact me, set meetings with me and want to do business with me. Sound familiar? Fortunately, I'd taken some internet marketing courses in the early 2000's when I started a different business that primarily used the internet. I knew what it took to rank for SEO, what platforms to use for building a decent looking website, how to write effective copy that would get people to take action, and where to spend the majority of my time to be most effective.

The very first day as a full time Real Estate Investor, I was receiving emails and phone calls from my ideal target market. I was getting homeowners wanting to book appointments and have me come and discuss the options available for their home. I was getting more leads in one month than most of my investor friends in a whole year.

From there, I went on to write 2 international #1 best-selling books in real estate investing, created 2 brands that are well known in the Canadian Real Estate Investing space, and built and sold marketing systems for other real estate investors. In addition, I created the marketing system and material for a nationwide rent to own company and coach real estate investors on how to generate more leads and opportunities for their business.

This example demonstrates that with the right tools, you can get yourself positioned very quickly and have great momentum in driving your business forward.

The big takeaway from all these examples is that before I even start helping people with my Authority Acceleration Blueprint or formula, I already had authority for myself from past experiences and accomplishments. I'm confident you can do exactly the same thing for yourself.

Don't think you can't be an authority quickly because you are just starting your business. Take what you have done and accomplished already, build on that and start communicating to your ideal target market with a message that resonates.

Chapter 4: Connection

CONNECTION

MESSAGES THAT RESONATE

con·nec·tion
noun
noun: **connection**; plural noun: **connections**;

a relationship in which a person, thing, or idea is linked or associated with something else.

"the couple has an amazing **connection**"

synonyms: link, relationship, relation,

Money's in the Message

One of the biggest hindrances to businesses selling more products and services is they don't really know their clients that well. Many of them never take the time to create an ideal customer avatar or determine what characteristics make up their very best customers. You know the ones who rave about you, your product, your services and even promote you to others. Those are the ones you want to attract more of into your business.

The businesses who say their customer is everyone are businesses that aren't going to be very successful. If you're trying to market your product or service to everyone, your message will get lost and resonate with no one.

How can you even begin to create messages, ads, or marketing material if you don't really know what makes your customer tick? This is one of the biggest mistakes businesses make when it comes to marketing. So many companies will just throw marketing messages out into the world hoping something sticks. Or worse yet, just blatantly ask for a sale without taking the time build a relationship and trust.

The reality is that nobody cares what you have to say, whether it's at a party, networking event or even a marketing message, unless it's relevant to them. Let's face it: there's so much noise in the world and so many people, brands and companies all vying for your attention, the messages that come at you each and every day don't register with your conscious mind. The same holds true for your potential clients. The only ones that really get through all the noise are the ones that make it through your "WIIFM" (what's in it for me) filter. In other words, the only ones you actually take notice of are brought to your conscious attention because there is some element that speaks directly to you or affects you in some way.

This means you've got to communicate in a very powerful way that immediately gets the attention of your ideal target market. In order to do this, you first must realize the product or service you sell to your ideal target market is only a means to an end for what they really want. It is their desired outcome.

Your customers aren't buying the features of the product or service your offer. They are buying the end result, their desired outcome and the benefits they receive from using your product or service. This means you want to focus on what you deliver, not what you do.

When you start to craft your messaging for your videos, interviews, live streaming, marketing, ads etc., focus on the end result – the benefits they will receive using your product or service, the problems your business helps them solve and eliminate any fears they may have you will help them overcome and the challenges they have faced up to this point.

A great exercise I learned from one of my past coaches is to ask yourself 3 simple questions with respect to your product or service. This aids you in positioning what you do from the perspective of the desired outcome or the benefits your ideal target market gets, instead of just describing your product or service. It also frames your offering in a way that is more compelling and relevant to your ideal target market.

- Q1. What I/We do is…

- Q2. What this means is…

- Q3. What this really means is…

When you become clear on what it really means, and you start using the terminology in your day to day conversations when people ask what you do, or in your messaging when creating videos, going live or crafting copy for your social posts or marketing material, you will discover a shift in the attention you start to get from your audience or the people you are communicating with.

Creating Value Through Questions

When it comes to getting people's attention and building authority, you will need to cut through the massive amount of communication and messaging people get each and every day if you want to reach your ideal target market. Everyone has their "WIIFM" filter turned on and they ask themselves, "Who are you and why should I listen to you?"

For your messages to be effective and resonate with your ideal target market, you need them to really connect and get past their "WIIFM" filter. One of the best methods to do that is to uncover and use their language, the language your ideal target market is currently using to have conversations in their mind. Next, identify the greatest decision triggers that make them buy. You can do this through surveys.

Surveying doesn't have to be complicated. It can be as simple as asking a series of questions that will provide you the feedback you're looking for. Below are a series of 6 questions that will get you the information you require to build your messages and get passed the "WIIFM" filter.

The first survey question should be based on the context of your market or the pain/problem they are trying to fix.

1. What is the single biggest fear you have when it comes to _____?

The word "biggest" focuses on one thing while fear is a very powerful emotion that drives most human behavior. This question helps uncover the real motivation and identifies why they aren't taking action.

An example would be "What is the single biggest fear you have when it comes to being recognized as the Authority?"

Some of the answers may be…
- I don't feel like I know enough

- People finding out I don't know it all

- I don't feel like I have enough experience

- I would have to speak or be interviewed

So in my messaging I would need to address and overcome their fears. Normally when you do a survey, you will get a number of different answers, but generally there will be 1 or 2 that stand out above all the rest. Those are the ones you will want focus on with your messaging. An example of some messaging may go something like this:

"When you implement the 'Authority Acceleration Blueprint' over the next 100 days, people will automatically recognize you as an Authority in your field of expertise even if you're just getting started. Don't feel like you know it all, or even have much experience."

The 2nd question is more about what really ticks people off or drives them crazy.

2. **What is the single biggest frustration you have when it comes to _____?**

The word "frustration" leads people to think about very emotional things and what really sets them off.

An example may be "What is the single biggest frustration you have when it comes to <u>positioning yourself as the authority</u>?

Some of the answers may be...

- I don't even know where to start

- It is very time consuming

- I am spending lots of money and not getting any results

- I don't understand all the internet marketing strategies

- I don't know which social platform I should focus on

- It takes a long time to get known in my industry

As mentioned above, I would want to focus on the top answers when I'm creating my messaging. An example of some messaging may go something like this:

Do all the social media platforms overwhelm you? Not sure where to spend your time to get the biggest impact and gain the most exposure for your business or brand? Are you burning though your advertising money not getting the Return On Investment you were looking for?

When you implement the "Authority Acceleration Blueprint" into your brand or business, you follow a very strategic step-by-step formula to minimize your time and maximize your exposure, which will position you as the Authority in your Field of Expertise in 100 days or less.

Now that you have recognized what your ideal target market's biggest fear, biggest frustration or biggest problem, it's time to ask them the following:

3. What's happening as a result of this (Problem/Frustration)?

Your goal here is to lead them to recognize their pain, fear or frustration and negative implications, so they connect their emotions with the problem or frustration they are experiencing.

Using the example, we discussed in number 2 as the problem/frustration, the answers may be as follows:

- Not doing anything

- Spending lots of time and it is ineffective

- Not growing my business

- Not increasing leads or sales

- Use traditional marketing strategies

- Have to lay off people

- Can't take holidays

As the marketer, you will want to use these answers to help you frame the need for a solution to what they realize has a big negative impact on their life. In reality you are connecting the emotion of what is happening, and the negative implications, back to the original problem. Take a look at the sample copy below…

At one time, I was there myself, just starting out in a new business and in a new field of expertise where very few people knew who I was or anything about me. The worst part was trying to get people to hire me or buy my services, so I had to give up taking holidays all together. I was spending a lot of time focused on the wrong strategies that weren't getting me the exposure and sales to make ends meet. I realized I had to get the right message, and myself, in front of more people if I wanted to grow my business, my brand, my income and grow my exposure; and that's what led me to create the Authority Acceleration Blueprint.

You now have tied the emotions of the negative impact back to the problem. It's time to ask the next question in the survey:

4. "What have you tried so far that hasn't worked?"

In most cases, they have probably tried things already that haven't worked. Knowing where they are will help you create messaging that will connect better with your ideal target market.

Keeping with our current theme of questions, here are some possible answers to that question:

- Posting on various social media
- Hired outsourcers for social media

- Networked at local groups
- Built sales funnel
- Facebook ads

If you know what these answers are and why they didn't work, then it will really allow you to target a solution that isn't something that most people think they've tried and isn't working. It really allows you to get into their head at some level and say "If you're like me..."

If you're like me, you've probably created a social media account on every platform, posting out links to sales pages, gone to local Meetup or Networking groups, built sales funnels and maybe even tried Facebook Ads, only to find you were spending way too much time and money doing all these things not getting the results you were looking for.

You now have connected with your audience all the things you have tried, which are probably similar to the things they've tried and failed at as well. Now, it's time to move on to the next question in the survey.

5. If a genie granted you the solution to this problem, what would the ideal solution be for you?

The idea of the genie in great because it removes all obstacles, objections and limitations people put on themselves as to why they can't do it or can't achieve their desired outcome. It takes away the 3 biggest obstacles people usually have, which are time, money and effort. You also want to be on the lookout for outrageous solutions so you aren't trying to sell an unrealistic solution.

Let's take a look at some possible answers to the example we have been working through in this chapter:

- I have a steady stream of clients wanting to work with me

- Everyone knows who I am and what I do

- People know exactly who I am and what I do, so I don't have to keep explaining myself

- I am attracting the right kind of people and repelling the wrong kind of people

- I am recognized as the authority and have lots of business

- I spend my time working with clients, not trying to find my next meal

Most people have something in the back of their mind they wish they could find in the market that solves their problem, but chances are if they are still looking they haven't found the right fit as of yet. By answering this question, they give you an insight into their wants and allow you to evaluate their expectations and understand their perspective. Take a look below for how you might use the answers in your copy.

Everyone knows you don't just wake up one morning and be a recognized authority where everyone knows who you are, what you do, and are lined up to work with you. Generally, it takes years of hard work and paying your dues to get to this point.

*IMAGINE being recognized as the authority in your business or field of expertise **100 days from today, and had clients lined up to work with you**. How great would it feel knowing that in 100 days you are a Recognized Best Selling Author, have Your Own Talk Show, as well as podcast, and you are only investing 1 hour a week of your time to create your authority content? If this describes you then you are in the right place…*

Now that you are aware of their ideal solution, it's time to ask the 6th and final question in the survey.

6. **What's the single biggest question you have when it comes to _____?"**

This question causes them to identify the highest value information for them, because they feel the answer to this question will give them the greatest traction for moving forward.

An example may be, "What is the single biggest question you have when it comes to <u>positioning yourself as the authority</u>?" Others to consider include:

- What's the most important thing I need to focus on?

- Do I need to be an author?

- Is there a certain amount of years of experience I need?

- Do I need to have certain education or qualifications?

- What's the fastest way to make it happen?

The answers you receive from the people you survey will become a powerful list of questions that you can use in your marketing. This list of questions will become a very key part of your packaging and promoting strategies as you move forward. The questions can be main topics for your videos, which will then get repurposed into articles, chapters in a book and much more. You're really going to be hitting the right market with this information as it's coming directly from your ideal target market. When you are incorporating these questions and provide the answers in your messaging and marketing, you will almost come across as psychic because you are answering the questions your market is asking.

Asking these 6 questions will uncover your ideal target market's decision triggers and the language they are using, which you will use in your marketing, messaging and when creating your content to create a powerful connection. By asking questions you show your dedication to really serving your market. Many of the people who answer the questions will thank you for taking the time to find out what they really think.

Now that you've gone through the foundation components of what it takes to create impact, become the authority and create a message that really connects with your audience, it's time to put this information into action and move on to Section 2 where you execute the acceleration of your authority status.

FREE Video

Authority Acceleration Formula

www.AuthorityAcceleratorCoach.com

Section 2: Execution

EXECUTION

----

ex·e·cu·tion
noun

the carrying out or putting into effect of a plan, order, or course of action.

"he was fascinated by the entire operation and its execution"

synonyms: implementation, carrying
out, accomplishment, bringing
off/about, engineering, attainment, realizati
on
"the execution of the plan"

Chapter 5: Strategy

STRATEGY

AUTHORITY ACCELERATION FORMULA

strat·e·gy
noun

a plan of action or policy designed to achieve a major
or overall aim.

"time to develop a coherent economic strategy"

synonyms: master plan, grand design, game
plan, plan (of action), action
plan, policy, program;
tactics; exit strategy

"the government's economic strategy"

Earlier in this book, I indicated that getting your message out to the masses so you can reach more people is hard, and it won't happen with just one livestream, video, image or post, that information has got to spread… or it won't be effective. So, it has to come out of you, and out into the open in a variety of different mediums, on a number of different platforms and on a consistent and persistent basis for other people to see, engage and share it with others.

I'm sure the question you are asking yourself right now is: "How do I do this and not spend all my time creating content like videos, books, podcasts, blogs, social posts etc.?"

The best way to get your information and messages out to the world most effectively and efficiently is by using a strategy or following a formula. Some of the greatest minds in the history of humans developed formulas to explain how things worked. They date as far back as 530BC when the Pythagorean Theory was created and the basis for our understanding of geometry started.

Then in 1687 Sir Isaac Newton figured out the Law of Gravity and why the planets act the way they do and how gravity works on earth. And let's not forget Albert Einstein's Theory of Relativity back in 1905 that gave us the relationship between Energy and Matter and the understanding of Space and Time.

What these individuals have done is break down the world around us and be able to explain it using a formula. Now, by no means do I think I'm a genius or come close to being in their category, but I've cracked the code and solved the problem that just about every person reading this book has right now. Yes, that's right…. It's getting more attention so you can build your brand, your business, your income, serve more people and make a bigger impact in people's lives in the shortest amount of time possible.

The good news is I've managed to boil it down and have developed a formula that, when implemented, consistently works. It's been tested across multiple industries, with large organizations and with the solo-preneurs. It took me over 5 years to refine and huge shifts in technology, the internet, and consumer behavior before this formula became clear.

AUTHORITY ACCELERATION FORMULA:

$$A^2 = [(x)LV + (y)RC + 10(x)DE] \times 100d$$

To most people, this formula looks daunting. Once we walk through the three main components of the formula, you will have a must better understanding of how all this comes together. If needed, Re-read this section. It is important to understand the formula before we move on and actually solve the equation.

Component 1:

$$A^2 = [(x)\underline{LV} + (y)RC + 10(x)DE] \times 100d$$

The first component of this formula is the **LV**, which stands for **Live Video**. It is more important than ever to create, produce and engage with others using live video, especially Facebook Live. When over 1 billion users on the planet are on Facebook, you can be guaranteed that your audience is hanging out there from time to time. Now, they may not always be there to catch your show or video live, but they can always watch the video afterwards.

When I talk to and coach my private clients, they all have the same 3 concerns, which were actually concerns I had for myself when I first started livestreaming:

1. I don't like myself on camera.

2. What am I going to say?

3. I don't know how to do it.

So I'm going to share with you the same thing I told myself and tell my clients:

- First, if you are delivering your talk, your video, and thinking about yourself, you need to check your ego. You are there to serve others, who only care about the value you deliver and the quality of the message, not whether you look like a model or not,

not how introverted or extroverted you are, or any other reason you tell yourself you can't do it. Make the video and the message about those you serve, not yourself.

- Second, I tried winging it on my videos early on... and you know what I discovered? I am AWFUL at hosting a live show that way. I forget things, I don't make calls to action when needed, I don't engage regularly... it was terrible. As a result, I built a show flow – the entire show scripted with calls to action, questions and when to engage with the audience.

- Third, when Facebook introduced its live stream video, it took the complexity out of doing livestreaming. You no longer need complicated equipment or software, all you need is your smart phone and a connection to the internet. Because of this, there is no longer any excuse why you shouldn't be creating live video to deliver your message and connect with your ideal target market.

Component 2:

$$A^2 = [(x)LV + (y)\textbf{\textit{RC}} + 10(x)DE] \times 100d$$

The second component of the formula I want to talk about is **RC**, which stands for **Repurposed Content.**

One of the greatest things I've learned from the experts I follow is this philosophy where your presence is always there and accessible on the internet. I'm a person who likes to be efficient and I love the idea of doing something once and then repurposing it on a variety of different mediums.

Here's an example of what gets created from The John A McCabe Show. Each 1-hour episode generates the following content:

- 1 Hour Video – Raw footage from the Facebook Live video
- Transcription of the show
- 1 Edited Video Podcast
- 1 Edited Audio Podcast
- 1 Chapter in an upcoming book
- 6-10 Video Clips for Social Media
- 2 Blog Articles for Website
- Notes for YouTube Page of uploaded video
- Notes for Website Page from Episode
- 10-20 Images and Social Posts

From the first half of The John A McCabe Show season, I have enough content for 70 video podcasts, 70 audio podcasts, content for 5 different books with 12-14 chapters each, over 130 blog articles, and over 1000 posts on all the major platforms. When it comes to doing it all, I have a tip that will help you get it all done without spending all your time and energy making it happen.

Outsource it!

Component 3:

$A^2 = [(x)LV + (y)RC + 10(x)\underline{\textit{DE}}] \times 100d$

The third and final major component of the formula is **DE**, which stands for **Distribution and Engagement**. This refers to taking your repurposed content and distributing it out to the internet world on a variety of social platforms, spending time engaging with people who engage on your content and seeking out others to engage on their content. This is all about giving value to others without asking for or expecting anything in return.

This means when people comment, share and like the content you share, you create a dialog with them without coming across as a salesman. It also means researching hashtags, influencers in your marketplace, groups, topics etc., and following, joining and engaging with others on their content. It is all about putting the Social back in Social Media.

As you will soon see, this is where the weight of this formula is placed, which is the exact opposite of what everyone is doing right now. Most people spend all their time creating content and very little on the distribution and engagement of that content. In reality, this is how and where you are going to gain the followers and people who get to know you, like you and trust you because they resonate with the message you share.

So, there you have the 3 main components that make up the formula. Now it is time to solve the equation that every single one of you can use and implement into your business and start accelerating your authority.

$$A^2 = [(x)LV + (y)RC + 10(x)DE] \times 100d$$

Formula Key:

A^2 = Rate of Your Authority Acceleration
x = hours per week you commit (1 is the minimum)
LV = Live Video
y = number of social platforms (4 is the minimum) –
LinkedIn, Facebook, Twitter, YouTube, Instagram, Pinterest, Snap Chat, Apple, Amazon
RC = Repurpose Content
DE = Distribution and Engagement
d = 1 day

What I'm going to do now is solve the equation that will help each and every one of you Accelerate Your Authority.

To solve the formula, we are going to use the minimums suggested in the formula key, which means that (x) = 1 hour per week and (y) = 4 platforms.

Here's the formula

$$A^2 = [(x)LV + (y)RC + 10(x)DE] \times 100d \text{ reads.}$$

The Rate at which you Accelerate Your Authority is equal to:

- Performing 1 hour per week of Live Video plus
- Repurposed Content that you can put on a minimum of 4 social platforms plus
- Performing 10 hours per week of Distributing and Engaging on the repurposed content
- Carried out for a total of 100 days.

So now, you have the formula and the solution, and know exactly what it will take to accelerate your authority over the next 100 days, to get you seen, get you heard, get you noticed, anywhere, anytime on any device.

One thing you should note: if you increase x or y, the rate at which you accelerate your authority goes up. For example, if you said $x = 5$ and $y = 7$, which is what I'm currently doing for The John A McCabe Show, it means I'm doing 5 hours of Live Video per week, repurposing my content for 7 different platforms – Facebook, YouTube, Twitter, Instagram, Amazon, Apple, Website, and I should be doing 50 hours per week of Distribution and Engagement.

I don't recommend creating that many hours of Live Video per week as it will create a bottle neck in the Repurposing Content and will make it hard to spend the appropriate amount of time Distributing and Engaging on the content.

I do recommend sticking to the 1 hour per week of Live video. Now that can be four 15 minute sessions, three 20 minute sessions, two 30 minute sessions or one 60-minute session. For most people, it is easier doing more sessions of a shorter duration.

So, start with that single video, tweet, picture, post from your phone and start your own ground swell. Use the ideas or thoughts you have, to educate the segment you serve and share your stories. It will be the start of something significant, and it will actually re-write your future.

It's really not the whole world that we have the power to change. What you can change is your mindset, your life, the world you have control over, your sphere, and I want to encourage you to do that. Because you know what? The future isn't a place that you're going to go to; it's a place that you get to create. And remember, the next 100 days are going to go by in a blink of an eye. Start today by taking some imperfect action on your journey to Accelerate Your Authority. It's about progress, not perfection.

In the next section, I've provided you a journal for planning and documenting your material and journey over the next 100 days. Take the tools you've learned from this book and plan, map out, and document your strategy over the next 100 days.

Chapter 6: Implementation

IMPLEMENTATION

----

im·ple·men·ta·tion

impləmən'tāSH(ə)n/

noun

noun: **implementation**; plural
noun: **implementations**

the process of putting a decision or plan into effect;
execution.

"she was responsible for the implementation of the
plan"

At this point you're asking yourself, "What do I do with this?"

Easy. Just do it.

Like anything in life that matters, it requires a little preparation and implementation.

The great news is there are resources available to help you with all the aspects discussed in this book.

I've been helping entrepreneurs, business owners, authors, experts and speakers grow their business, their brand, their income, their exposure, serve more people and make a bigger impact in people's lives for year.

I can help you, too – and the training you need to learn more and get started is free. To access the free information, visit

www.AuthorityAcceleratorCoach.com/Masterclass

I look forward to hearing about your success and I will see you on the other side of the screen!

100 Day Journal

Document your first 25 Days within this book. You can download the full 100 Day Journal by visiting

Bit.ly/100DayP

100 Day Journal

Download the FULL 100-Day Authority Acceleration Planner…

FREE Download

100-Day Authority Acceleration Planner visit: Bit.ly/100DayP

---

100 Day Journal

Day 1 Planner

This Weeks Main Goal: Actions to Take Today that will move me closer to my goal

1. _____
2. _____
3. _____
4. _____
5. _____

Live Video Planned for today:

Time: _____
Length: _____
Topic: _____
Notes: _____

Show Flow:

Segment	Approx Length	Graphics/Files	Notes

Repurposing Content – Indicate what you will create from the repurposed content today for: **Enter "RC" in the Cell**
Distribution: Indicate where you will distribute content today:
Enter a "D" in the Cell

	Facebook	Youtube	Twitter	Instagram	LinkedIn	iTunes	Website
Transcripts							
Video Clips							
Images							
Quotes							
Video Podcast							
Audio Podcast							
Blog Article							
Long Form Article							
Book Content							

Distribution and Engagement:

	Research (hashtags/influencers)	Engage (Yours/Others Content)
Time Allocated:		
Findings		
Notes		

100 Day Journal

Day 2 Planner

This Weeks Main Goal: Actions to Take Today that will move me closer to my goal

1. _____
2. _____
3. _____
4. _____
5. _____

Live Video Planned for today:

Time: _____

Length: _____

Topic: _____

Notes: _____

Show Flow:

Segment	Approx Length	Graphics/Files	Notes

Repurposing Content – Indicate what you will create from the repurposed content today for: **Enter "RC" in the Cell**
Distribution: Indicate where you will distribute content today: **Enter a "D" in the Cell**

	Facebook	Youtube	Twitter	Instagram	LinkedIn	iTunes	Website
Transcripts							
Video Clips							
Images							
Quotes							
Video Podcast							
Audio Podcast							
Blog Article							
Long Form Article							
Book Content							

Distribution and Engagement:

	Research (hashtags/influencers)	Engage (Yours/Others Content)
Time Allocated:		
Findings		
Notes		

100 Day Journal

Day 3 Planner

This Weeks Main Goal: Actions to Take Today that will move me closer to my goal

1. _____
2. _____
3. _____
4. _____
5. _____

Live Video Planned for today:

Time: _____
Length: _____
Topic: _____
Notes: _____

Show Flow:

Segment	Approx Length	Graphics/Files	Notes

Repurposing Content – Indicate what you will create from the repurposed content today for: **Enter "RC" in the Cell**
Distribution: Indicate where you will distribute content today:
Enter a "D" in the Cell

	Facebook	Youtube	Twitter	Instagram	LinkedIn	iTunes	Website
Transcripts							
Video Clips							
Images							
Quotes							
Video Podcast							
Audio Podcast							
Blog Article							
Long Form Article							
Book Content							

Distribution and Engagement:

	Research (hashtags/influencers)	Engage (Yours/Others Content)
Time Allocated:		
Findings		
Notes		

100 Day Journal

Day 4 Planner

This Weeks Main Goal: Actions to Take Today that will move me closer to my goal

1. _____
2. _____
3. _____
4. _____
5. _____

Live Video Planned for today:

Time: _____

Length: _____

Topic: _____

Notes: _____

Show Flow:

Segment	Approx Length	Graphics/Files	Notes

Repurposing Content – Indicate what you will create from the repurposed content today for: **Enter "RC" in the Cell**
Distribution: Indicate where you will distribute content today:
Enter a "D" in the Cell

	Facebook	Youtube	Twitter	Instagram	LinkedIn	iTunes	Website
Transcripts							
Video Clips							
Images							
Quotes							
Video Podcast							
Audio Podcast							
Blog Article							
Long Form Article							
Book Content							

Distribution and Engagement:

	Research (hashtags/influencers)	Engage (Yours/Others Content)
Time Allocated:		
Findings		
Notes		

100 Day Journal

Day 5 Planner

This Weeks Main Goal: Actions to Take Today that will move me closer to my goal

1. _____
2. _____
3. _____
4. _____
5. _____

Live Video Planned for today:

Time: _____

Length: _____

Topic: _____

Notes: _____

Show Flow:

Segment	Approx Length	Graphics/Files	Notes

Repurposing Content – Indicate what you will create from the repurposed content today for: **Enter "RC" in the Cell**
Distribution: Indicate where you will distribute content today: **Enter a "D" in the Cell**

	Facebook	Youtube	Twitter	Instagram	LinkedIn	iTunes	Website
Transcripts							
Video Clips							
Images							
Quotes							
Video Podcast							
Audio Podcast							
Blog Article							
Long Form Article							
Book Content							

Distribution and Engagement:

	Research (hashtags/influencers)	Engage (Yours/Others Content)
Time Allocated:		
Findings		
Notes		

100 Day Journal

Day 6 Planner

This Weeks Main Goal: Actions to Take Today that will move me closer to my goal

1. _____
2. _____
3. _____
4. _____
5. _____

Live Video Planned for today:

Time: _____

Length: _____

Topic: _____

Notes: _____

Show Flow:

Segment	Approx Length	Graphics/Files	Notes

Repurposing Content – Indicate what you will create from the repurposed content today for: **Enter "RC" in the Cell**

Distribution: Indicate where you will distribute content today: **Enter a "D" in the Cell**

	Facebook	Youtube	Twitter	Instagram	LinkedIn	iTunes	Website
Transcripts							
Video Clips							
Images							
Quotes							
Video Podcast							
Audio Podcast							
Blog Article							
Long Form Article							
Book Content							

Distribution and Engagement:

	Research (hashtags/influencers)	Engage (Yours/Others Content)
Time Allocated:		
Findings		
Notes		

100 Day Journal

Day 7 Planner

This Weeks Main Goal: Actions to Take Today that will move me closer to my goal

1. _____
2. _____
3. _____
4. _____
5. _____

Live Video Planned for today:

Time: _____
Length: _____
Topic: _____
Notes: _____

Show Flow:

Segment	Approx Length	Graphics/Files	Notes

Repurposing Content – Indicate what you will create from the repurposed content today for: **Enter "RC" in the Cell**
Distribution: Indicate where you will distribute content today:
Enter a "D" in the Cell

	Facebook	Youtube	Twitter	Instagram	LinkedIn	iTunes	Website
Transcripts							
Video Clips							
Images							
Quotes							
Video Podcast							
Audio Podcast							
Blog Article							
Long Form Article							
Book Content							

Distribution and Engagement:

	Research (hashtags/influencers)	Engage (Yours/Others Content)
Time Allocated:		
Findings		
Notes		

100 Day Journal

Day 8 Planner

This Weeks Main Goal: Actions to Take Today that will move me closer to my goal

1. _____
2. _____
3. _____
4. _____
5. _____

Live Video Planned for today:

Time: _____

Length: _____

Topic: _____

Notes: _____

Show Flow:

Segment	Approx Length	Graphics/Files	Notes

Repurposing Content – Indicate what you will create from the repurposed content today for: **Enter "RC" in the Cell**
Distribution: Indicate where you will distribute content today:
Enter a "D" in the Cell

	Facebook	Youtube	Twitter	Instagram	LinkedIn	iTunes	Website
Transcripts							
Video Clips							
Images							
Quotes							
Video Podcast							
Audio Podcast							
Blog Article							
Long Form Article							
Book Content							

Distribution and Engagement:

	Research (hashtags/influencers)	Engage (Yours/Others Content)
Time Allocated:		
Findings		
Notes		

100 Day Journal

Day 9 Planner

This Weeks Main Goal: Actions to Take Today that will move me closer to my goal

1. _____
2. _____
3. _____
4. _____
5. _____

Live Video Planned for today:

Time: _____
Length: _____
Topic: _____
Notes: _____

Show Flow:

Segment	Approx Length	Graphics/Files	Notes

Repurposing Content – Indicate what you will create from the repurposed content today for: **Enter "RC" in the Cell**
Distribution: Indicate where you will distribute content today:
Enter a "D" in the Cell

	Facebook	Youtube	Twitter	Instagram	LinkedIn	iTunes	Website
Transcripts							
Video Clips							
Images							
Quotes							
Video Podcast							
Audio Podcast							
Blog Article							
Long Form Article							
Book Content							

Distribution and Engagement:

	Research (hashtags/influencers)	Engage (Yours/Others Content)
Time Allocated:		
Findings		
Notes		

100 Day Journal

Day 10 Planner

This Weeks Main Goal: Actions to Take Today that will move me closer to my goal

1. _____
2. _____
3. _____
4. _____
5. _____

Live Video Planned for today:

Time: _____
Length: _____
Topic: _____
Notes: _____

Show Flow:

Segment	Approx Length	Graphics/Files	Notes

Repurposing Content – Indicate what you will create from the repurposed content today for: **Enter "RC" in the Cell**
Distribution: Indicate where you will distribute content today:
Enter a "D" in the Cell

	Facebook	Youtube	Twitter	Instagram	LinkedIn	iTunes	Website
Transcripts							
Video Clips							
Images							
Quotes							
Video Podcast							
Audio Podcast							
Blog Article							
Long Form Article							
Book Content							

Distribution and Engagement:

	Research (hashtags/influencers)	Engage (Yours/Others Content)
Time Allocated:		
Findings		
Notes		

100 Day Journal

Day 11 Planner

This Weeks Main Goal: Actions to Take Today that will move me closer to my goal

1. _____
2. _____
3. _____
4. _____
5. _____

Live Video Planned for today:

Time: _____
Length: _____
Topic: _____
Notes: _____

Show Flow:

Segment	Approx Length	Graphics/Files	Notes

Repurposing Content – Indicate what you will create from the repurposed content today for: **Enter "RC" in the Cell**
Distribution: Indicate where you will distribute content today:
Enter a "D" in the Cell

	Facebook	Youtube	Twitter	Instagram	LinkedIn	iTunes	Website
Transcripts							
Video Clips							
Images							
Quotes							
Video Podcast							
Audio Podcast							
Blog Article							
Long Form Article							
Book Content							

Distribution and Engagement:

	Research (hashtags/influencers)	Engage (Yours/Others Content)
Time Allocated:		
Findings		
Notes		

100 Day Journal

Day 12 Planner

This Weeks Main Goal: Actions to Take Today that will move me closer to my goal

1. _____
2. _____
3. _____
4. _____
5. _____

Live Video Planned for today:

Time: _____

Length: _____

Topic: _____

Notes: _____

Show Flow:

Segment	Approx Length	Graphics/Files	Notes

Repurposing Content – Indicate what you will create from the repurposed content today for: **Enter "RC" in the Cell**
Distribution: Indicate where you will distribute content today: **Enter a "D" in the Cell**

	Facebook	Youtube	Twitter	Instagram	LinkedIn	iTunes	Website
Transcripts							
Video Clips							
Images							
Quotes							
Video Podcast							
Audio Podcast							
Blog Article							
Long Form Article							
Book Content							

Distribution and Engagement:

	Research (hashtags/influencers)	Engage (Yours/Others Content)
Time Allocated:		
Findings		
Notes		

100 Day Journal

Day 13 Planner

This Weeks Main Goal: Actions to Take Today that will move me closer to my goal

1. _____
2. _____
3. _____
4. _____
5. _____

Live Video Planned for today:

Time: _____

Length: _____

Topic: _____

Notes: _____

Show Flow:

Segment	Approx Length	Graphics/Files	Notes

Repurposing Content – Indicate what you will create from the repurposed content today for: **Enter "RC" in the Cell**
Distribution: Indicate where you will distribute content today: **Enter a "D" in the Cell**

	Facebook	Youtube	Twitter	Instagram	LinkedIn	iTunes	Website
Transcripts							
Video Clips							
Images							
Quotes							
Video Podcast							
Audio Podcast							
Blog Article							
Long Form Article							
Book Content							

Distribution and Engagement:

	Research (hashtags/influencers)	Engage (Yours/Others Content)
Time Allocated:		
Findings		
Notes		

100 Day Journal

Day 14 Planner

This Weeks Main Goal: Actions to Take Today that will move me closer to my goal

1. _____
2. _____
3. _____
4. _____
5. _____

Live Video Planned for today:
Time: _____
Length: _____
Topic: _____
Notes: _____

Show Flow:

Segment	Approx Length	Graphics/Files	Notes

Repurposing Content – Indicate what you will create from the repurposed content today for: **Enter "RC" in the Cell**
Distribution: Indicate where you will distribute content today: **Enter a "D" in the Cell**

	Facebook	Youtube	Twitter	Instagram	LinkedIn	iTunes	Website
Transcripts							
Video Clips							
Images							
Quotes							
Video Podcast							
Audio Podcast							
Blog Article							
Long Form Article							
Book Content							

Distribution and Engagement:

	Research (hashtags/influencers)	Engage (Yours/Others Content)
Time Allocated:		
Findings		
Notes		

100 Day Journal

Day 15 Planner

This Weeks Main Goal: Actions to Take Today that will move me closer to my goal

1. _____
2. _____
3. _____
4. _____
5. _____

Live Video Planned for today:

Time: _____
Length: _____
Topic: _____
Notes: _____

Show Flow:

Segment	Approx Length	Graphics/Files	Notes

Repurposing Content – Indicate what you will create from the repurposed content today for: **Enter "RC" in the Cell**
Distribution: Indicate where you will distribute content today: **Enter a "D" in the Cell**

	Facebook	Youtube	Twitter	Instagram	LinkedIn	iTunes	Website
Transcripts							
Video Clips							
Images							
Quotes							
Video Podcast							
Audio Podcast							
Blog Article							
Long Form Article							
Book Content							

Distribution and Engagement:

	Research (hashtags/influencers)	Engage (Yours/Others Content)
Time Allocated:		
Findings		
Notes		

100 Day Journal

Day 16 Planner

This Weeks Main Goal: Actions to Take Today that will move me closer to my goal

1. _____
2. _____
3. _____
4. _____
5. _____

Live Video Planned for today:

Time: _____
Length: _____
Topic: _____
Notes: _____

Show Flow:

Segment	Approx Length	Graphics/Files	Notes

Repurposing Content – Indicate what you will create from the repurposed content today for: **Enter "RC" in the Cell**
Distribution: Indicate where you will distribute content today: **Enter a "D" in the Cell**

	Facebook	Youtube	Twitter	Instagram	LinkedIn	iTunes	Website
Transcripts							
Video Clips							
Images							
Quotes							
Video Podcast							
Audio Podcast							
Blog Article							
Long Form Article							
Book Content							

Distribution and Engagement:

	Research (hashtags/influencers)	Engage (Yours/Others Content)
Time Allocated:		
Findings		
Notes		

100 Day Journal

Day 17 Planner

This Weeks Main Goal: Actions to Take Today that will move me closer to my goal

1. _____
2. _____
3. _____
4. _____
5. _____

Live Video Planned for today:
Time: _____
Length: _____
Topic: _____
Notes: _____

Show Flow:

Segment	Approx Length	Graphics/Files	Notes

Repurposing Content – Indicate what you will create from the repurposed content today for: **Enter "RC" in the Cell**
Distribution: Indicate where you will distribute content today: **Enter a "D" in the Cell**

	Facebook	Youtube	Twitter	Instagram	LinkedIn	iTunes	Website
Transcripts							
Video Clips							
Images							
Quotes							
Video Podcast							
Audio Podcast							
Blog Article							
Long Form Article							
Book Content							

Distribution and Engagement:

	Research (hashtags/influencers)	Engage (Yours/Others Content)
Time Allocated:		
Findings		
Notes		

100 Day Journal

Day 18 Planner

This Weeks Main Goal: Actions to Take Today that will move me closer to my goal

1. _____
2. _____
3. _____
4. _____
5. _____

Live Video Planned for today:

Time: _____

Length: _____

Topic: _____

Notes: _____

Show Flow:

Segment	Approx Length	Graphics/Files	Notes

Repurposing Content – Indicate what you will create from the repurposed content today for: **Enter "RC" in the Cell**
Distribution: Indicate where you will distribute content today:
Enter a "D" in the Cell

	Facebook	Youtube	Twitter	Instagram	LinkedIn	iTunes	Website
Transcripts							
Video Clips							
Images							
Quotes							
Video Podcast							
Audio Podcast							
Blog Article							
Long Form Article							
Book Content							

Distribution and Engagement:

	Research (hashtags/influencers)	Engage (Yours/Others Content)
Time Allocated:		
Findings		
Notes		

100 Day Journal

Day 19 Planner

This Weeks Main Goal: Actions to Take Today that will move me closer to my goal

1. _____
2. _____
3. _____
4. _____
5. _____

Live Video Planned for today:

Time: _____
Length: _____
Topic: _____
Notes: _____

Show Flow:

Segment	Approx Length	Graphics/Files	Notes

Repurposing Content – Indicate what you will create from the repurposed content today for: **Enter "RC" in the Cell Distribution:** Indicate where you will distribute content today: **Enter a "D" in the Cell**

	Facebook	Youtube	Twitter	Instagram	LinkedIn	iTunes	Website
Transcripts							
Video Clips							
Images							
Quotes							
Video Podcast							
Audio Podcast							
Blog Article							
Long Form Article							
Book Content							

Distribution and Engagement:

	Research (hashtags/influencers)	Engage (Yours/Others Content)
Time Allocated:		
Findings		
Notes		

100 Day Journal

Day 20 Planner

This Weeks Main Goal: Actions to Take Today that will move me closer to my goal

1. _____
2. _____
3. _____
4. _____
5. _____

Live Video Planned for today:

Time: _____

Length: _____

Topic: _____

Notes: _____

Show Flow:

Segment	Approx Length	Graphics/Files	Notes

Repurposing Content – Indicate what you will create from the repurposed content today for: **Enter "RC" in the Cell**
Distribution: Indicate where you will distribute content today: **Enter a "D" in the Cell**

	Facebook	Youtube	Twitter	Instagram	LinkedIn	iTunes	Website
Transcripts							
Video Clips							
Images							
Quotes							
Video Podcast							
Audio Podcast							
Blog Article							
Long Form Article							
Book Content							

Distribution and Engagement:

	Research (hashtags/influencers)	Engage (Yours/Others Content)
Time Allocated:		
Findings		
Notes		

100 Day Journal

Day 21 Planner

This Weeks Main Goal: Actions to Take Today that will move me closer to my goal

1. _____
2. _____
3. _____
4. _____
5. _____

Live Video Planned for today:

Time: _____
Length: _____
Topic: _____
Notes: _____

Show Flow:

Segment	Approx Length	Graphics/Files	Notes

Repurposing Content – Indicate what you will create from the repurposed content today for: **Enter "RC" in the Cell**
Distribution: Indicate where you will distribute content today:
Enter a "D" in the Cell

	Facebook	Youtube	Twitter	Instagram	LinkedIn	iTunes	Website
Transcripts							
Video Clips							
Images							
Quotes							
Video Podcast							
Audio Podcast							
Blog Article							
Long Form Article							
Book Content							

Distribution and Engagement:

	Research (hashtags/influencers)	Engage (Yours/Others Content)
Time Allocated:		
Findings		
Notes		

100 Day Journal

Day 22 Planner

This Weeks Main Goal: Actions to Take Today that will move me closer to my goal

1. _____
2. _____
3. _____
4. _____
5. _____

Live Video Planned for today:

Time: _____
Length: _____
Topic: _____
Notes: _____

Show Flow:

Segment	Approx Length	Graphics/Files	Notes

Repurposing Content – Indicate what you will create from the repurposed content today for: **Enter "RC" in the Cell**
Distribution: Indicate where you will distribute content today: **Enter a "D" in the Cell**

	Facebook	Youtube	Twitter	Instagram	LinkedIn	iTunes	Website
Transcript s							
Video Clips							
Images							
Quotes							
Video Podcast							
Audio Podcast							
Blog Article							
Long Form Article							
Book Content							

Distribution and Engagement:

	Research (hashtags/influencers)	Engage (Yours/Others Content)
Time Allocated:		
Findings		
Notes		

100 Day Journal

Day 23 Planner

This Weeks Main Goal: Actions to Take Today that will move me closer to my goal

1. _____
2. _____
3. _____
4. _____
5. _____

Live Video Planned for today:

Time: _____

Length: _____

Topic: _____

Notes: _____

Show Flow:

Segment	Approx Length	Graphics/Files	Notes

Repurposing Content – Indicate what you will create from the repurposed content today for: **Enter "RC" in the Cell**
Distribution: Indicate where you will distribute content today: **Enter a "D" in the Cell**

	Facebook	Youtube	Twitter	Instagram	LinkedIn	iTunes	Website
Transcripts							
Video Clips							
Images							
Quotes							
Video Podcast							
Audio Podcast							
Blog Article							
Long Form Article							
Book Content							

Distribution and Engagement:

	Research (hashtags/influencers)	Engage (Yours/Others Content)
Time Allocated:		
Findings		
Notes		

100 Day Journal

Day 24 Planner

This Weeks Main Goal: Actions to Take Today that will move
me closer to my goal

1. _____
2. _____
3. _____
4. _____
5. _____

Live Video Planned for today:

Time: _____
Length: _____
Topic: _____
Notes: _____

Show Flow:

Segment	Approx Length	Graphics/Files	Notes

Repurposing Content – Indicate what you will create from the repurposed content today for: **Enter "RC" in the Cell**
Distribution: Indicate where you will distribute content today:
Enter a "D" in the Cell

	Facebook	Youtube	Twitter	Instagram	LinkedIn	iTunes	Website
Transcripts							
Video Clips							
Images							
Quotes							
Video Podcast							
Audio Podcast							
Blog Article							
Long Form Article							
Book Content							

Distribution and Engagement:

	Research (hashtags/influencers)	Engage (Yours/Others Content)
Time Allocated:		
Findings		
Notes		

100 Day Journal

Day 25 Planner

This Weeks Main Goal: Actions to Take Today that will move me closer to my goal

1. _____
2. _____
3. _____
4. _____
5. _____

Live Video Planned for today:

Time: _____
Length: _____
Topic: _____
Notes: _____

Show Flow:

Segment	Approx Length	Graphics/Files	Notes

Repurposing Content – Indicate what you will create from the repurposed content today for: **Enter "RC" in the Cell**
Distribution: Indicate where you will distribute content today: **Enter a "D" in the Cell**

	Facebook	Youtube	Twitter	Instagram	LinkedIn	iTunes	Website
Transcripts							
Video Clips							
Images							
Quotes							
Video Podcast							
Audio Podcast							
Blog Article							
Long Form Article							
Book Content							

Distribution and Engagement:

	Research (hashtags/influencers)	Engage (Yours/Others Content)
Time Allocated:		
Findings		
Notes		

Download the FULL 100-Day
Authority Acceleration Planner.....

FREE Download

100-Day Authority
Acceleration Planner

visit: Bit.ly/100DayP

FREE Video
Authority Acceleration Formula

www.AuthorityAcceleratorCoach.com

FREE Masterclass

Create Authority That Sells. How to Get Their Attention and Turn Them into Clients

www.AuthorityAcceleratorCoach.com/Masterclass

www.ingramcontent.com/pod-product-compliance
Lightning Source LLC
Chambersburg PA
CBHW071159200326
41519CB00018B/5288